Englisch-Stars

3

Erarbeitet von

Barbara Gleich
Irene Reindl
Katrin Schmidt
Britta Schöpe

Illustriert von

Martina Mair und
Wilfried Poll

Inhalt

1. Fill in.

Hello, my name is Sally. What's your name?

My name is John.

And what's your _____ ?

My _____

123 2. Number in the correct order. ✓

◯ My name is John.

◯ My name is Sally. What's your name?

◯ Hello. What's your name?

Nummeriere in der richtigen Reihenfolge.

3

✎ 3. What do they say? Write. ☑

Schreibe in die richtigen Sprechblasen.

Good night.
Good afternoon.
Good evening.
Good morning.

1. Find the words and draw lines.

Finde die Wörter und kreise sie ein. Verbinde dann mit dem richtigen Bild.

bluegreenblackpurplewhitepinkyellowredgreybrownorange

2. What's Sally's favourite colour? Do the crossword.

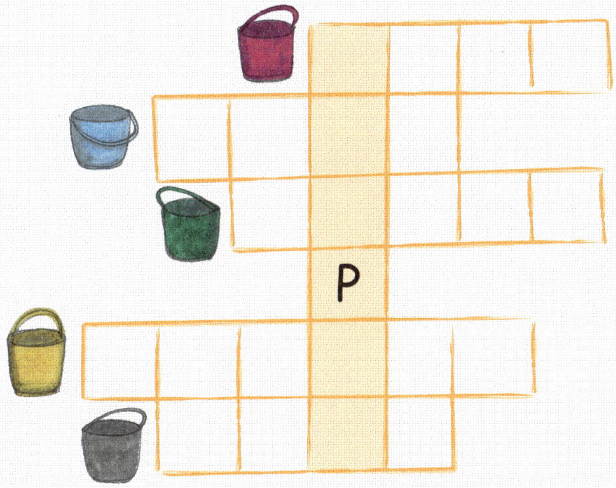

Finde Sallys Lieblingsfarbe heraus.

P

grey
yellow
blue
green
pink

My favourite colour is

_____.

5

 3. Draw lines.

Verbinde mit den richtigen Farben. Achtung, zu zwei Bildern gehören mehrere Farben.

grey

blue

black

green

red

brown

yellow

 4. Write and colour.

l r u p p e

h i w e t

e n e r g

e d r

r y g e

l l w y o e

yellow

green

white

red

purple

grey

Was soll das denn heißen?

Da sind Buchstaben durcheinandergekommen. Schreibe erst das Wort, male dann den Pinsel in der richtigen Farbe an.

5. Find the words and circle them. ✔

Suche die Wörter senkrecht und waagrecht. Kreise ein.

y	m	a	b	j	l	g
e	o	g	r	e	e	n
l	r	g	o	h	b	h
l	a	e	w	d	l	a
o	n	a	n	v	u	u
w	g	a	g	r	e	y
r	e	d	c	u	k	p
f	g	n	i	z	h	u
o	b	w	h	i	t	e

orange   brown
green   yellow
red   white
grey   blue

6. What colour is missing? Write. ✔

Welche Farben fehlen? Schreibe die Wörter in der richtigen Farbe dazu.

red + blue = _____

_____ + blue = green

yellow + _____ = orange

black + white = _____

7

1. Write the numbers in the correct order.

_____

_____

_____

_____

_____

Da sollen wir bestimmt die Zahlen in der richtigen Reihenfolge aufschreiben.

nine

two

five

one

six

three

four

eight

seven

ten

2. Count and write. ✓

Wie viele Fische gibt es von jeder Art?

8

Oh, was ist denn hier passiert?
Aber du kannst das Wort sicher noch einmal richtig aufschreiben.

3. Do you know the word? Write. ✓

nine → _____

five → _____

seven → _____

one → _____

eight → _____

ten → _____

4. How many lollies? Trace the lines and write. ✓

Fahre die Linien nach. Wie viele Lollis bekommt jeder? Schreibe die Zahlen als Wörter.

_____ lollies

_____ lollies

_____ lollies

_____ lollies

Jetzt kannst du schon auf Englisch rechnen. Schreibe die Ergebnisse als Wörter.

5. How much is it? Write. ✔ ❓

three + one = _____   ten – seven = _____

two + five = _____   five – four = _____

three + six = _____   seven – five = _____

four + one = _____   nine – eight = _____

6. Correct or wrong? Tick. ✔

Richtig oder falsch? Mache einen Haken.

	correct	wrong
There are **two** .	⚪	⚪
There is **one** .	⚪	⚪
There are **eight** .	⚪	⚪
There are **seven** .	⚪	⚪

 1. Number. ✓

Ordne den Schulsachen die richtige Zahl zu.

1. schoolbag
2. book
3. folder
4. ruler
5. pencil case
6. pencil
7. rubber
8. scissors
9. glue

2. Draw lines. ✓

lollipop lady
board
teacher
chalk
desk
pen
picture
poster
computer

11

Jeweils ein Wort in der Reihe passt nicht. Streiche es durch.

3. Odd one out. ✓

rubber – ruler – girl – computer

pen – scissors – pencil – song

board – chalk – five – desk

book – boy – teacher – pupil

 4. Read, look and write. What's missing?

Was sollen die Kinder alles aus ihrer Schultasche nehmen? Auf jedem Tisch fehlt etwas.

Take out your folder, a pencil, a rubber, glue and scissors.

What's missing on Steve's desk?

The _____ is missing.

What's missing on Kathy's desk?

The _____ is missing.

What's missing on Polly's desk?

The _____ is missing.

5. Read and colour.

The pencil case is green.

The ruler is yellow.

The pen is red.

The pencil is blue.

The rubber is pink.

The lollipop is purple.

Male in der richtigen Farbe aus.

6. What belongs in the schoolbag? Write.

pencil	scissors	ruler
desk	chalk	pencil case
poster	folder	board
pen	computer	glue
book	rubber	

Schreibe auf, was in die Schultasche gehört.

13

Finde die Wörter senkrecht
und waagrecht. Kreise sie ein.
Trage sie dann unten richtig ein.

1. Find the words and circle them. Fill in.

n	b	o	d	y	t	u	r	z	l	u	q
s	h	a	n	d	s	x	c	b	e	l	v
f	a	w	a	r	m	s	p	y	g	m	h
e	s	q	r	b	m	l	o	p	s	y	a
e	c	v	e	f	o	o	t	a	b	u	i
t	h	y	b	t	j	k	h	w	e	f	r
z	e	h	l	a	e	y	e	s	k	l	p
w	a	y	f	i	n	g	e	r	s	c	n
b	d	m	n	q	r	u	h	l	p	q	o
w	d	g	h	m	m	o	u	t	h	y	s
d	e	a	r	s	g	t	o	e	s	y	e
g	h	a	k	n	e	e	s	l	o	p	g

☑

body	hair
foot	ears
feet	toes
head	hands
legs	nose
arms	mouth
eyes	knees
fingers	

I've got 2 _____ .

I've got 2 _____ and 10 _____ .

I see with my _____ .

I hear with my _____ .

I smell with my _____ .

I speak with my _____ .

I've got 2 _____ and 2 _____ .

This is 1 _____ and these are 2 _____ .

And I've got 10 _____ .

14

✏️ 2. How do they feel? Draw lines and write. ✅

How do you
feel, Jack?

I'm _____ .

I want to eat a sandwich.

How do you
feel, Susan?

I'm _____ .

It's my birthday.

How do you
feel, Sam?

I'm _____ .

I don't like spiders.

happy

sad

hungry

angry

scared

tired

fine

How do you
feel, Jim?

I'm _____ .

I broke my arm.

How do you
feel, Annie?

I'm _____ .

I can't watch TV.

How do you
feel, Maggie?

I'm _____ .

I want to go to bed.

How do you feel, Liz?

I'm _____ , thank you.

3. Which alien is it? Read and number. ☑

Alien number one has got two heads, five legs and three arms.
It's happy.

Alien number two has got two heads, two noses and one big ear.
It's angry.

Alien number three has got one head, four eyes and one mouth with
two teeth.

Alien number four has got one head, five feet, one ear and one arm.

Alien number five has got _____ arms, _____

legs, _____ fingers and _____ noses.

1. What is it? Draw lines and write.

   teddy bear

castle

   inline skates

lorry

racing car

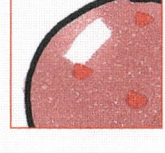   computer game

   doll

helicopter

   ball

spaceship

2. Do the crossword.

3. At the toy shop.
Match the pictures to the speech bubbles. Draw lines and fill in.

Verbinde die Bilder mit den richtigen Sprechblasen. Ergänze dann den Text.

It's _____ £.

Hello, can I help you?

Thank you. Goodbye.

I like this _____.

How much is it?

18

4. Trace the lines and write.

Katie buys a _____ . It's _____ £.

Ken buys a _____ . It's _____ £.

Anne buys a _____ . It's _____ £.

Derek buys a _____ . It's _____ £.

Betty buys a _____ . It's _____ £.

racing car   teddy bear   helicopter   doll   spaceship

1. Such a long scarf! Find the words. Draw lines and write. ✓

skirttrouserspulloverbootscapsocksshirt

Ein Bild bleibt übrig.
Welches Wort fehlt?
Schreibe es auf.

_____ , _____ , _____ ,

_____ , _____ , _____ ,

_____   This word is missing: _____

2. Look and write. ✓

Jenny puts on her _____ ,

her _____

and her _____ .

Brian takes off his _____ , his

_____ and his _____ .

| shoes | gloves | scarf | dress | woolly hat | anorak |

20

3. What can you see? Write.

shoes – a pullover –
a skirt – a jacket

Spure jeweils nur die Wörter für die Kleidungsstücke nach, die abgebildet sind.

a pair of trousers –
a pullover –
a T-shirt – a dress

a pair of shorts –
socks – a T-shirt –
a pullover

4. Dress Janet and Jack. Write. ?

Suche Kleidung für Janet und Jack aus. Schreibe auf.

Janet: _____

_____

Jack: _____

_____

 5. Funny . Read and tick. ✓

It's wearing…

○ a woolly hat, a jacket, a pair of trousers and shoes.

○ a cap, a scarf, a jacket, a pair of shorts and boots.

○ a cap, a scarf, an anorak, a pair of trousers and shoes.

It's wearing…

○ a woolly hat, a pullover, a pair of trousers and gloves.

○ a cap, an anorak, a T-shirt, a pair of shorts and boots.

○ a jacket, a woolly hat, socks, a pair of trousers and shoes.

It's wearing…

○ gloves, a woolly hat, a shirt, a skirt and boots.

○ gloves, a scarf, a woolly hat, a pullover and a pair of trousers.

○ a T-shirt, a dress, a cap, a pair of shorts and shoes.

Schau aus den Fenstern.
Beschreibe das Wetter.

1. Look outside the windows. What's the weather like? Write.

It's _____ .

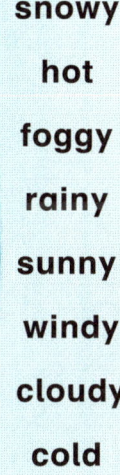

snowy

hot

foggy

rainy

sunny

windy

cloudy

cold

It's _____
and _____ .

It's _____
and _____ .

It's _____
and _____
and _____ .

 2. Odd one out.

| snowy – cold – hot | | sunny – cloudy – rainy |

| sunny – hot – snowy | | windy – hot – rainy |

3. Fill in the missing letters. Draw lines and write. ✓

Ergänze zuerst die fehlenden Buchstaben der Wochentage. Verbinde dann die Wochentage mit den passenden Bildern und schreibe auf.

1. ☐ onday

2. ☐ uesday

3. Wednes ☐ ☐ ☐

4. Thursday

5. ☐ riday

6. ☐ atur ☐ ☐ ☐

7. Su ☐ day

On __Monday__ it's __sunny__ .

On _____ it's _____ .

On _____ it's _____ .

_____ .

_____ .

_____ .

On _____ it's _____

and _____ .

Thursday	Monday	Friday	Tuesday	Saturday	Wednesday

Sunday	sunny	rainy (2x)	foggy	windy	snowy	cloudy (2x)

4. Read the comic.

Crazy weather

SUNDAY

MONDAY

On TUESDAY Sally puts on a T-shirt and shorts...

WEDNESDAY

On THURSDAY it's windy.

FRIDAY

But on SATURDAY Sally is prepared...

25

 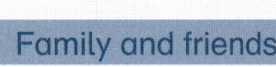

 1. Draw lines and write. ✓

mother   father

sister   grandmother

brother   grandfather

_____

_____

 2. Look and write. ✓

grandpa
grandma
mum
dad

_____ _____

Kennst du auch
die englischen
Kosenamen?

_____ _____

 3. Find the words and write. Then solve the riddles. ✔

Mike's family tree

grandpa   grandma

uncle   aunt

Mike

He's my mum's dad.
He's my grandpa.

She's my dad's mum.
She's my ⬚⬚⬚⬚⬚⬚ .

She's my dad's sister.
She's my ⬚⬚⬚⬚ .

He's my mum's brother.
He's my ⬚⬚⬚⬚ .

Vervollständige erst den Familienstamm-baum. Löse dann die Rätsel.

 4. Read and write. ☑

JOHN   LUCY   BEN   ANNA

 My best friend has got long brown hair. She is wearing a pink pullover.

My best friend is _____ .

 My best friend is a boy. He has got short blond hair and is wearing a pair of grey shorts.

My best friend is _____ .

 My best friend has got brown hair. She likes her inline skates very much.

My best friend is _____ .

 My best friend is wearing a blue T-shirt. He has got black hair.

My best friend is _____ .

And that's my best friend!

  5. An interview. Read and fill in.

my brother Joe and
my brother Tom

my sister Helen

my friend David

Sam, 9 years

: Hello. What's your name?

: My name is _____ .

: How old are you?

: I'm _____ years old.

: Have you got brothers?

: Yes. I have got _____ , Joe and Tom.

: And how many sisters have you got?

: I have got _____ . Her name is _____ .

: Who is your best friend?

: My best _____ is _____ .

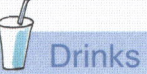

Trage zu jedem Wort die richtige Nummer ein und spure nach.

1. Number and write. ✔

○ hot chocolate
○ coffee
○ tea
○ orange juice
○ milk
○ coke
○ lemonade
○ water
○ apple juice

2. Find the words and circle them. What's missing? ✔

Finde die Wörter. Die Bilder helfen dir. Ein Bild bleibt übrig. Welches Wort fehlt? Schreibe es auf.

```
m o s  water  g l u c o k e
t e a z w l e m o n a d e b n
t u n a p p l e j u i c e m m
p m u c o f f e e w e m i l k
o s s h o t c h o c o l a t e s
```

This word is missing: _____

3. Look and write. ✔ ?

My favourite drink

is _____ .

My favourite drink

is _____ .

My favourite drink

is _____ .

My favourite drink

is _____ .

My favourite drink

is _____ .

My favourite drink

is _____ .

My favourite drink

is _____

_____ .

My favourite drink

is _____

_____ .

My favourite drink

is _____

_____ .

| hot chocolate | coffee | tea | orange juice | milk |
| coke | lemonade | water | apple juice |

✏ 1. Look and write.

cornflakes	honey	bacon	egg	jam	roll	butter
	bread	toast	ham			

✏ 2. Find the words and write. ✔

r _____ ll   _____

b _____ n   _____

e _____   _____

corn _____ s   _____

ho _____ y   _____

folgen vielfältige Übungen zur Wort-
olung und -sicherung sowie zur
Lese- und Schreibvermögens, z.B.
fgaben, Bilderrätsel und Dialoge.
s mit Sally zeigen den Kindern, wie
selbstständig lesen und verstehen

fgabenstellungen und Selbstkontrol-
Lösungsteil ermöglichen den Kindern,
nit den Englisch-Stars zu arbeiten.

im Picture dictionary, nach jedem
besonders schwierige Aufgaben
gaben) dürfen sich die Kinder mit
en-Aufkleber belohnen. Als beson-
rgeben die Sterne am Ende des
samtbild.

Stars dienen der spielerischen und
useinandersetzung mit Englisch und
eude am Erlernen der Fremdsprache.

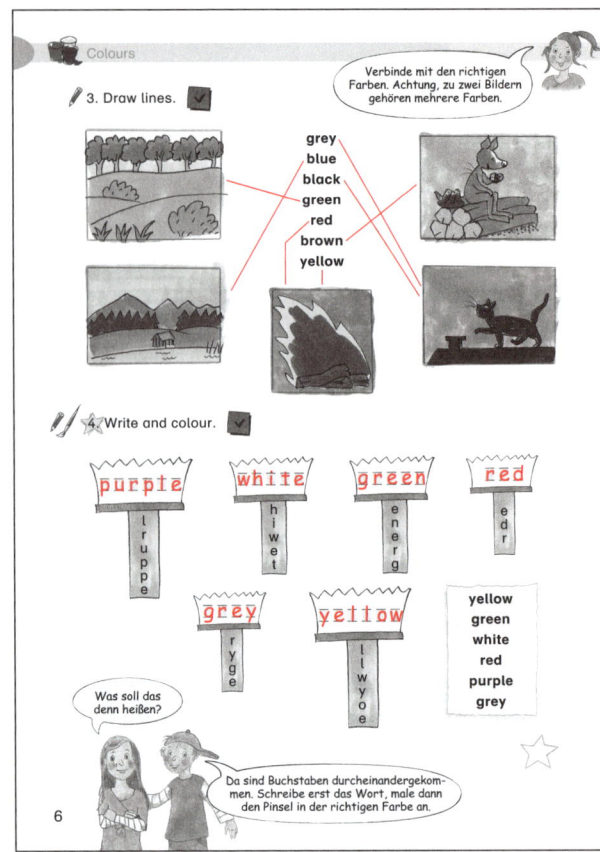

Colours

3. Draw lines. ✓

Verbinde mit den richtigen Farben. Achtung, zu zwei Bildern gehören mehrere Farben.

grey
blue
black
green
red
brown
yellow

4. Write and colour. ✓

purple
t r u p p e

white
h i w e t

green
e n e r g

red
e d r

grey
r y g e

yellow
l l w y o e

yellow
green
white
red
purple
grey

Was soll das denn heißen?

Da sind Buchstaben durcheinandergekommen. Schreibe erst das Wort, male dann den Pinsel in der richtigen Farbe an.

6

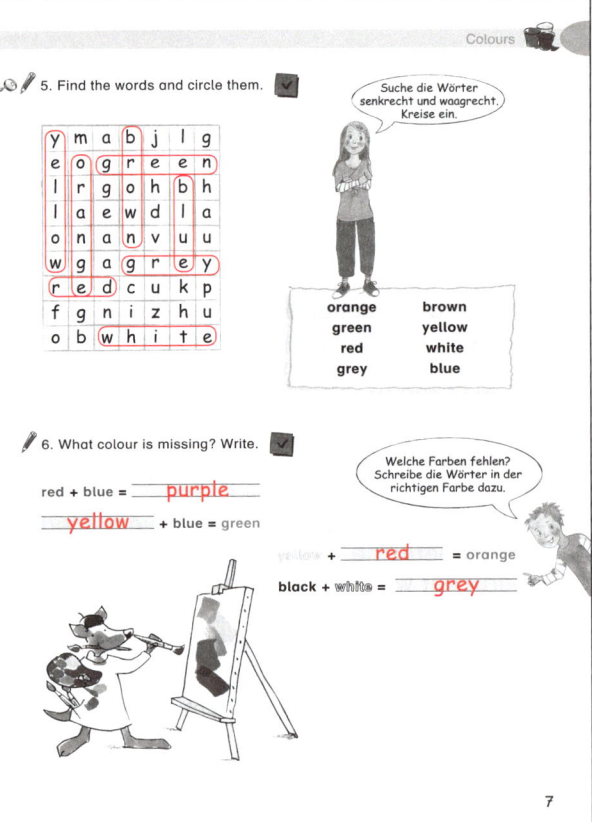

Colours

5. Find the words and circle them. ✓

Suche die Wörter senkrecht und waagrecht. Kreise ein.

y	m	a	b	j	l	g
e	o	g	r	e	e	n
l	r	g	o	h	b	h
l	a	e	w	d	l	a
o	n	a	n	v	u	u
w	g	a	g	r	e	y
r	e	d	c	u	k	p
f	g	n	i	z	h	u
o	b	w	h	i	t	e

orange   brown
green   yellow
red   white
grey   blue

6. What colour is missing? Write. ✓

Welche Farben fehlen? Schreibe die Wörter in der richtigen Farbe dazu.

red + blue = purple

yellow + blue = green

yellow + red = orange

black + white = grey

7

1/6 Numbers

1. Write the numbers in the correct order.

one, two, three, four,
five, six, seven, eight,
nine, ten

Da sollen wir bestimmt die Zahlen in der richtigen Reihenfolge aufschreiben.

nine
two
five
one
six
three
eight
four
seven
ten

2. Count and write. ✓

Wie viele Fische gibt es von jeder Art?

eight three five six

8

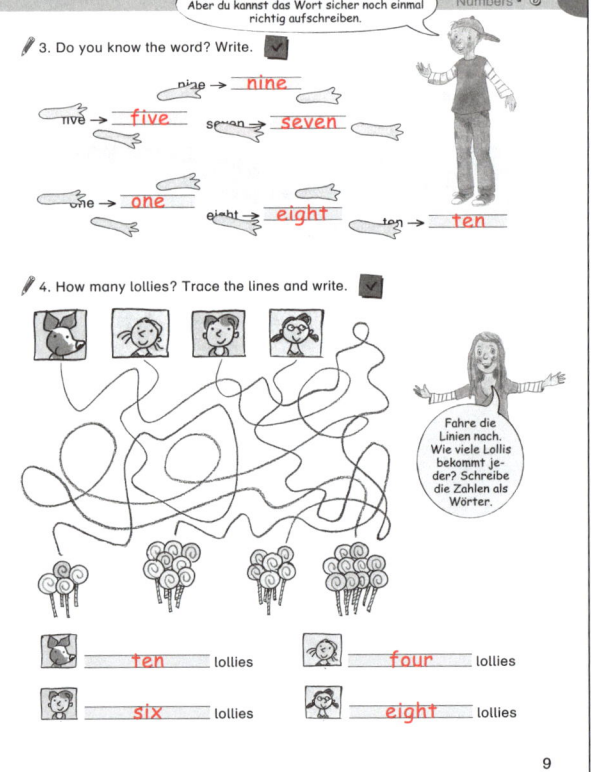

Oh, was ist denn hier passiert? Aber du kannst das Wort sicher noch einmal richtig aufschreiben.

Numbers 1/6

3. Do you know the word? Write. ✓

nine → nine
five → five
seven → seven
one → one
eight → eight
ten → ten

4. How many lollies? Trace the lines and write. ✓

Fahre die Linien nach. Wie viele Lollis bekommt jeder? Schreibe die Zahlen als Wörter.

ten lollies
four lollies
six lollies
eight lollies

9

1⁷₆ Numbers

5. How much is it? Write. ✓ ?

Jetzt kannst du schon auf Englisch rechnen. Schreibe die Ergebnisse als Wörter.

three + one = __four__   ten – seven = __three__

two + five = __seven__   five – four = __one__

three + six = __nine__   seven – five = __two__

four + one = __five__   nine – eight = __one__

6. Correct or wrong? Tick. ✓

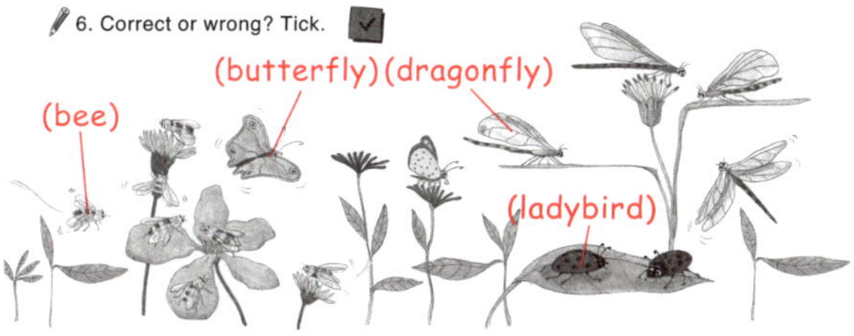

(butterfly) (dragonfly)

(bee)

(ladybird)

Richtig oder falsch? Mache einen Haken.

	correct	wrong
There are **two** .	✓	
There is **one** .		✓
There are **eight** .		✓
There are **seven** .	✓	

10

At school

1₂3 1. Number. ✓

Ordne den Schulsachen die richtige Zahl zu.

⑤ ④ ⑥ ⑧ ⑦ ② ③ ⑨ ①

1. schoolbag
2. book
3. folder
4. ruler
5. pencil case
6. pencil
7. rubber
8. scissors
9. glue

2. Draw lines. ✓

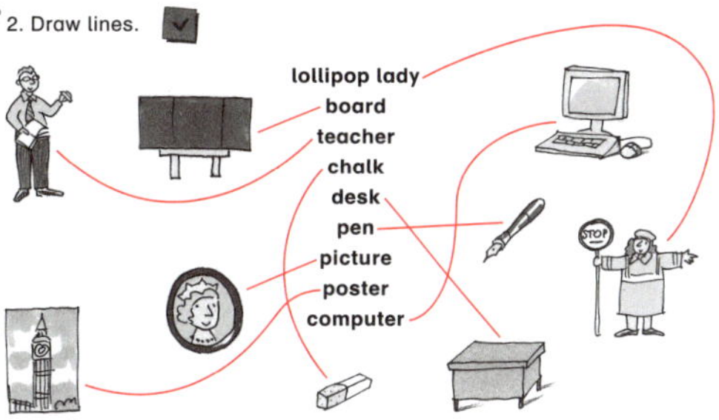

lollipop lady
board
teacher
chalk
desk
pen
picture
poster
computer

11

At school

3. Odd one out. ✓

Jeweils ein Wort in der Reihe passt nicht. Streiche es durch.

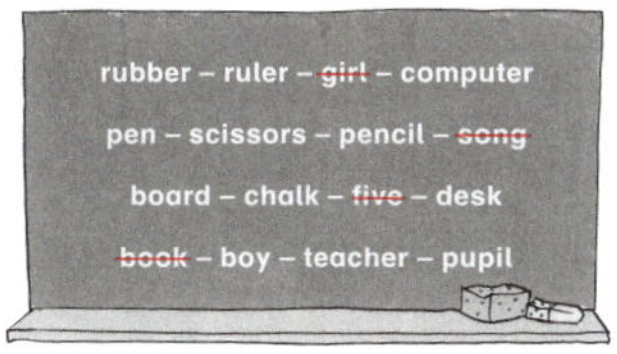

rubber – ruler – ~~girl~~ – computer

pen – scissors – pencil – ~~song~~

board – chalk – ~~five~~ – desk

~~book~~ – boy – teacher – pupil

4. Read, look and write. What's missing? ✓

Take out your folder, a pencil, a rubber, glue and scissors.

Was sollen die Kinder alles aus ihrer Schultasche nehmen? Auf jedem Tisch fehlt etwas.

What's missing on Steve's desk?

The __pencil__ is missing.

What's missing on Kathy's desk?

The __rubber__ is missing.

What's missing on Polly's desk?

The __folder__ is missing.

12

At school

5. Read and colour. ✓ (blau)

The pencil case is green.

The ruler is yellow.

The pen is red.

The pencil is blue.

The rubber is pink.

The lollipop is purple.

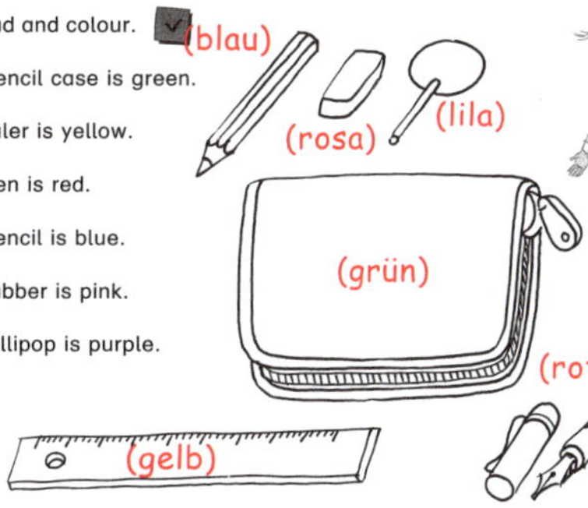

(rosa) (lila)

Male in der richtigen Farbe aus.

(grün)

(rot)

(gelb)

6. What belongs in the schoolbag? Write. ✓ ?

pencil	scissors	ruler
desk	chalk	pencil case
poster	folder	board
pen	computer	glue
book	rubber	

__book, folder, glue, pen, pencil,__
__pencil case, rubber, ruler,__
__scissors__

Schreibe auf, was in die Schultasche gehört.

13

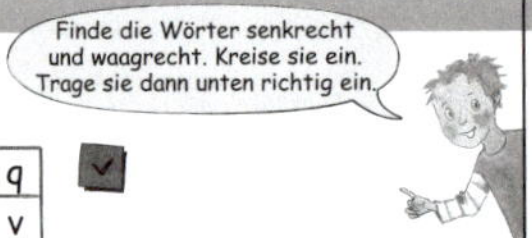

Lösungen

1. Find the words and circle them. Fill in.

Finde die Wörter senkrecht und waagrecht. Kreise sie ein. Trage sie dann unten richtig ein.

n	b	o	d	y	t	u	r	z	l	u	q
s	h	a	n	d	s	x	c	b	e	l	v
f	a	w	a	r	m	s	p	y	g	m	h
e	s	q	r	b	m	l	o	p	s	y	a
e	c	v	e	f	o	o	t	a	b	u	i
t	h	y	b	t	j	k	h	w	e	f	r
z	e	h	l	a	e	y	e	s	k	l	p
w	a	y	f	i	n	g	e	r	s	c	n
b	d	m	n	q	r	u	h	l	p	q	o
w	d	g	h	m	o	u	t	h	y	s	
d	e	a	r	s	g	t	o	e	s	y	e
g	h	a	k	n	e	e	s	l	o	p	g

body	hair
foot	ears
feet	toes
head	hands
legs	nose
arms	mouth
eyes	knees
fingers	

I've got 2 __arms__ .

I've got 2 __hands__ and 10 __fingers__ .

I see with my __eyes__ .

I hear with my __ears__ .

I smell with my __nose__ .

I speak with my __mouth__ .

I've got 2 __legs__ and 2 __knees__ .

This is 1 __foot__ and these are 2 __feet__ .

And I've got 10 __toes__ .

14

---

2. How do they feel? Draw lines and write.

How do you feel, Jack? 
I'm __hungry__ .
I want to eat a sandwich.

How do you feel, Susan? 
I'm __happy__ .
It's my birthday.

How do you feel, Sam?
I'm __scared__ .
I don't like spiders.

happy
sad
hungry
angry
scared
tired
fine

How do you feel, Jim?
I'm __sad__ .
I broke my arm.

How do you feel, Annie? 
I'm __angry__ .
I can't watch TV.

How do you feel, Maggie? 
I'm __tired__ .
I want to go to bed.

How do you feel, Liz?
I'm __fine__ , thank you.

15

---

3. Which alien is it? Read and number.

Alien number one has got two heads, five legs and three arms. It's happy.

Alien number two has got two heads, two noses and one big ear. It's angry.

Alien number three has got one head, four eyes and one mouth with two teeth.

Alien number four has got one head, five feet, one ear and one arm.

Alien number five has got __four__ arms, __three__ legs, __four__ fingers and __two__ noses.

16

---

1. What is it? Draw lines and write.

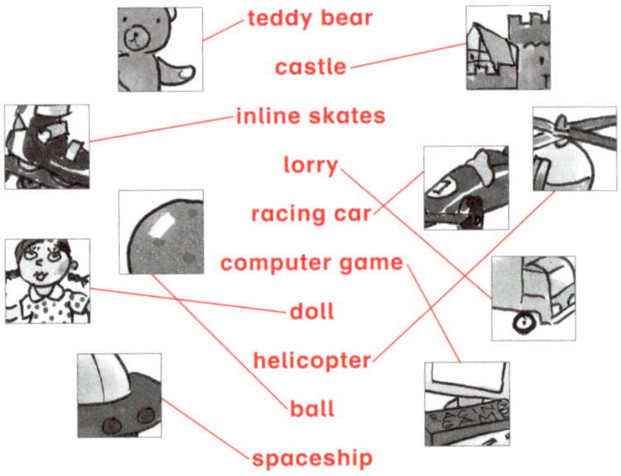

teddy bear
castle
inline skates
lorry
racing car
computer game
doll
helicopter
ball
spaceship

2. Do the crossword.

R A C I N G C A R
B A L L
S P A C E S H I P
T E D D Y B E A R
D O L L
H E L I C O P T E R

17

Toys

3. At the toy shop.
Match the pictures to the speech bubbles. Draw lines and fill in.

Verbinde die Bilder mit den richtigen Sprechblasen. Ergänze dann den Text.

It's _four_ £.

Hello, can I help you?

I like this _lorry_ How much is it?

Thank you. Goodbye.

18

Toys

4. Trace the lines and write.

Katie   Ken   Anne   Derek   Betty

5 £   6 £   8 £   4 £   10 £

Katie buys a _doll_. It's 4 (four) £.
Ken buys a _racing car_. It's 8 (eight) £.
Anne buys a _spaceship_. It's 6 (six) £.
Derek buys a _helicopter_. It's 10 (ten) £.
Betty buys a _teddy bear_. It's 5 (five) £.

| racing car | teddy bear | helicopter | doll | spaceship |

19

Clothes

1. Such a long scarf! Find the words. Draw lines and write.

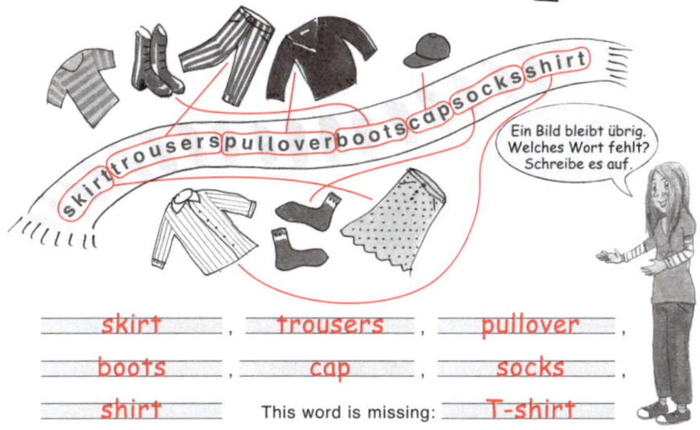

skirt trousers pullover boots cap socks shirt

Ein Bild bleibt übrig. Welches Wort fehlt? Schreibe es auf.

skirt, _trousers_, _pullover_,
boots, _cap_, _socks_,
shirt   This word is missing: _T-shirt_

2. Look and write.

Jenny puts on her _dress_,
her _anorak_
and her _shoes_.
Brian takes off his _woolly hat_, his
gloves and his _scarf_

| shoes | gloves | scarf | dress | woolly hat | anorak |

20

Clothes

3. What can you see? Write.

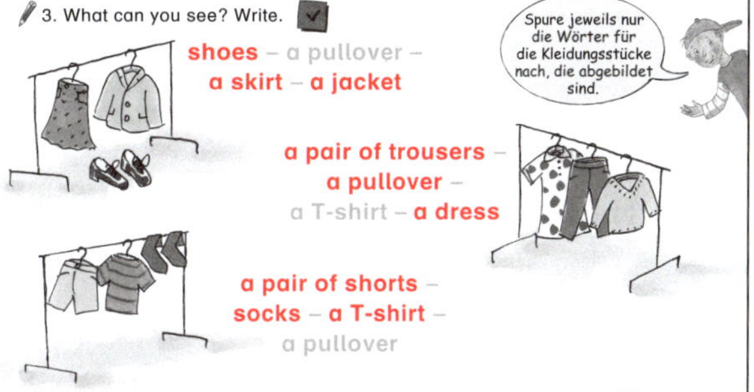

shoes – a pullover – a skirt – a jacket

a pair of trousers – a pullover – a T-shirt – a dress

a pair of shorts – socks – a T-shirt – a pullover

Spure jeweils nur die Wörter für die Kleidungsstücke nach, die abgebildet sind.

4. Dress Janet and Jack. Write.

Suche Kleidung für Janet und Jack aus. Schreibe auf.

(mögliche Lösung)
Janet: a skirt, a T-Shirt, socks, (pink) shoes, a woolly hat, a scarf, a jacket
Jack: a pair of trousers, a shirt, gloves, a cap, a pullover, (brown) shoes, an anorak, socks

21

Lösungen

5. Funny ___. Read and tick. ✓

It's wearing…
- ○ a woolly hat, a jacket, a pair of trousers and shoes.
- ✓ a cap, a scarf, a jacket, a pair of shorts and boots.
- ○ a cap, a scarf, an anorak, a pair of trousers and shoes.

It's wearing…
- ○ a woolly hat, a pullover, a pair of trousers and gloves.
- ○ a cap, an anorak, a T-shirt, a pair of shorts and boots.
- ✓ a jacket, a woolly hat, socks, a pair of trousers and shoes.

It's wearing…
- ✓ gloves, a woolly hat, a shirt, a skirt and boots.
- ○ gloves, a scarf, a woolly hat, a pullover and a pair of trousers.
- ○ a T-shirt, a dress, a cap, a pair of shorts and shoes.

22

Schau aus den Fenstern. Beschreibe das Wetter.

1. Look outside the windows. What's the weather like? Write. ✓

snowy
hot
foggy
rainy
sunny
windy
cloudy
cold

It's __foggy__ .

It's __sunny__
and __hot__ .

It's __snowy__
and __cold__ .

It's __cloudy__
and __windy__
and __rainy__ .

2. Odd one out. ✓

snowy – cold – ~~hot~~

~~sunny~~ – cloudy – rainy

sunny – hot – ~~snowy~~

windy – ~~hot~~ – rainy

23

---

3. Fill in the missing letters. Draw lines and write. ✓

Ergänze zuerst die fehlenden Buchstaben der Wochentage. Verbinde dann die Wochentage mit den passenden Bildern und schreibe auf.

1. Monday
2. Tuesday
3. Wednesday
4. Thursday
5. Friday
6. Saturday
7. Sunday

On __Monday__ it's __sunny__ .
On __Tuesday__ it's __foggy__ .
On __Wednesday__ it's __windy__ .
On Thursday it's snowy .
On Friday it's rainy .
On Saturday it's cloudy .
On __Sunday__ it's __cloudy__
and __rainy__ .

| Thursday | Monday | Friday | Tuesday | Saturday | Wednesday |
| Sunday | sunny | rainy (2x) | foggy | windy | snowy | cloudy (2x) |

24

---

4. Read the comic. ?

Crazy weather

SUNDAY — On Monday it's snowy.

MONDAY

On TUESDAY Sally puts on a T-shirt and shorts…

On Wednesday it's sunny.

WEDNESDAY

On THURSDAY it's windy.

On Friday it's sunny and warm.

FRIDAY

But on SATURDAY Sally is prepared…

25

1. Draw lines and write.

mother — father
sister — grandmother
brother — grandfather

mother, sister, brother, father,
grandmother, grandfather

2. Look and write.

grandpa
grandma
mum
dad

mum   dad
grandma    grandpa

Kennst du auch die englischen Kosenamen?

26

3. Find the words and write. Then solve the riddles.

Mike's family tree

grandpa grandma   grandpa grandma
uncle mum   dad aunt
sister   brother

He's my mum's dad.
He's my grandpa.
She's my dad's mum.
She's my grandma.

She's my dad's sister.
She's my aunt.

He's my mum's brother.
He's my uncle.

Vervollständige erst den Familienstammbaum. Löse dann die Rätsel.

27

4. Read and write.

JOHN LUCY BEN ANNA

My best friend has got long brown hair. She is wearing a pink pullover.
My best friend is Lucy.

My best friend is a boy. He has got short blond hair and is wearing a pair of grey shorts.
My best friend is Ben.

My best friend has got brown hair. She likes her inline skates very much.
My best friend is Anna.

My best friend is wearing a blue T-shirt. He has got black hair.
My best friend is John.

And that's my best friend!

28

5. An interview. Read and fill in.

my brother Joe and my brother Tom    my sister Helen    my friend David

Sam, 9 years

: Hello. What's your name?
: My name is Sam.
: How old are you?
: I'm nine years old.
: Have you got brothers?
: Yes. I have got two brothers, Joe and Tom.
: And how many sisters have you got?
: I have got one sister. Her name is Helen.
: Who is your best friend?
: My best friend is David.

29

Lösungen

1. Number and write. ✓

- (3) hot chocolate
- (8) coffee
- (2) tea
- (9) orange juice
- (4) milk
- (6) coke
- (5) lemonade
- (1) water
- (7) apple juice

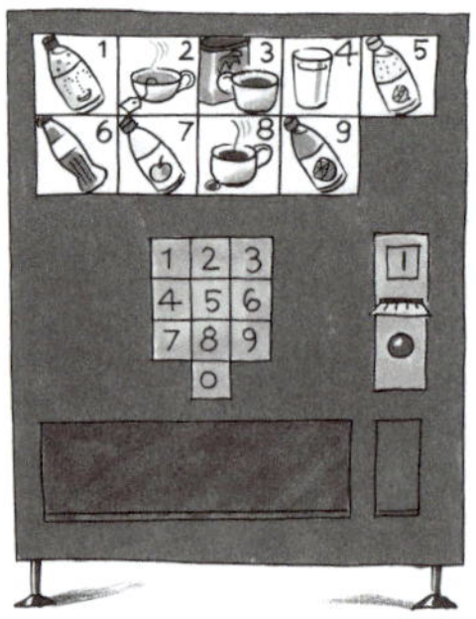

Trage zu jedem Wort die richtige Nummer ein und spure nach.

2. Find the words and circle them. What's missing? ✓

```
m o s w a t e r g l u c o k e
t e a z w l e m o n a d e b n
t u n a p p l e j u i c e m m
p m u c o f f e e w e m i l k
o s s h o t c h o c o l a t e s
```

Finde die Wörter. Die Bilder helfen dir. Ein Bild bleibt übrig. Welches Wort fehlt? Schreibe es auf.

This word is missing: **orange juice**

30

3. Look and write. ✓ ?

My favourite drink is **coke**.
My favourite drink is **lemonade**.
My favourite drink is **coffee**.

My favourite drink is **milk**.
My favourite drink is **water**.
My favourite drink is **tea**.

My favourite drink is **orange juice**.
My favourite drink is **apple juice**.
My favourite drink is **hot chocolate**.

hot chocolate	coffee	tea	orange juice	milk
coke	lemonade	water	apple juice	

31

1. Look and write. ✓ ?

Breakfast

- toast
- honey
- bread
- ham
- roll
- bacon
- butter
- egg
- jam
- cornflakes

cornflakes	honey	bacon	egg	jam	roll	butter
bread	toast	ham				

2. Find the words and write. ✓

- r_ll **roll**
- b_n **bacon**
- e_ **egg**
- corn_s **cornflakes**
- ho_y **honey**

32

3. Read and draw lines. ✓

I like cornflakes with milk for breakfast.

I like a roll with jam and hot chocolate for breakfast.

I like bacon and eggs and orange juice for breakfast.

I like toast with honey and milk for breakfast.

4. What's missing? Read and draw. ✓

I have toast with jam and a glass of orange juice for breakfast.

I have a roll with ham and a glass of milk for breakfast.

(Schinken)

(Orangensaft)

I have bread with butter, an egg and a cup of tea for breakfast.

(Ei)

Ergänze die Bilder.

33

Page 34

Breakfast

1. 3. 5. Read and number. ✔ ?

Findest du heraus, wer an welchem Platz sitzt?

I don't like cornflakes, but I like coffee. ②

I like toast, but I don't like hot chocolate. ③

I don't like toast. ①   I don't like ham. ④

6. Crazy breakfast. What's wrong? Write. ✔

Irgendwie sind die Sätze durcheinandergeraten. Schreibe sie richtig auf.

I like a roll with tea and a cup of jam.
I like a roll with jam and a cup of tea.

I like toast with cornflakes and honey with milk.
I like toast with honey and cornflakes with milk.

I like bread with orange juice and a glass of ham.
I like bread with ham and a glass of orange juice.

34

Page 35

Fruit

1. Do the crossword. ✔

M E L O N
P L U M
B A N A N A   C
P I N E A P P L E
S T R A W B E R R Y
O R A N G E

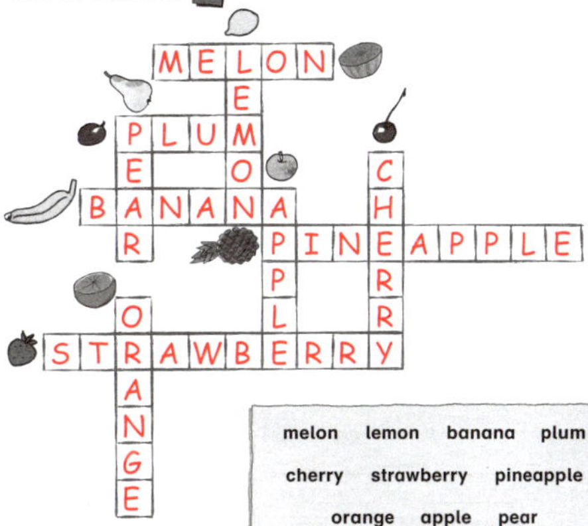

melon   lemon   banana   plum
cherry   strawberry   pineapple
orange   apple   pear

2. Find the five fruit in the basket. Write. ✔

banana
lemon
melon
pear
pineapple

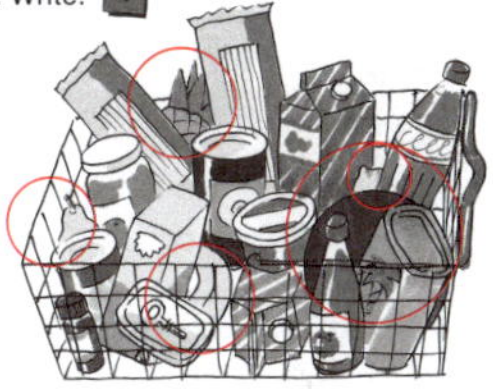

35

Page 36

Fruit

Wörter mit –y am Ende schreibe ich in der Mehrzahl mit –ies. Wie bei cherry – cherries.

3. Trace the lines and write. ✔

Dave   Sarah   Emily   Tim   Mary

Dave likes plums.
Sarah likes **strawberries**.
Emily likes **oranges**.
Tim likes **apples**.
Mary likes **cherries**.

strawberries   cherries   apples   plums   oranges

4. Guess the fruit and write. ✔

a p p l e   m e l o n

banana
pear
melon
apple

p e a r   b a n a n a

36

Page 37

Fruit

5. Read the comic. ?

Yummy fruit juices

Hello.

Hello. Would you like a fruit juice?

apple juice
lemon juice
pineapple juice
plum juice
strawberry-banana juice
melon-pear juice
orange juice
cherry juice
£1

Yes, an apple juice, please. No, sorry. A strawberry-banana juice, please.

No, sorry! A pineapple juice.

You can have a fruit juice with all the fruit.

No, sorry! A lemon juice.

That's great!

No, sorry! A plum juice.

That's £ 1, please.

Thank you! Yummy! I love this fruit juice!!!

Here you are.

37

Lösungen

1. What pet is it? Write and draw lines.

budgie   cat
dog   fish
guinea pig
hamster   mouse
rabbit   tortoise

My pet is red. It can swim.
It's a __fish__ .

My pet is black. It says "miaow".
It's a __cat__ .

My pet is blue. It can fly.
It's a __budgie__ .

My pet is brown and white. It's very small.
It's a __hamster__ .

My pet is brown. It says "bow-wow".
It's a __dog__ .

My pet is black and white. It likes apples.
It's a __guinea pig__ .

My pet is green. It has got short legs.
It's a __tortoise__ .

My pet is white. It has got long ears.
It's a __rabbit__ .

And my pet is a mouse.

38

2. Find the pets and colour the fields green. What can you see?

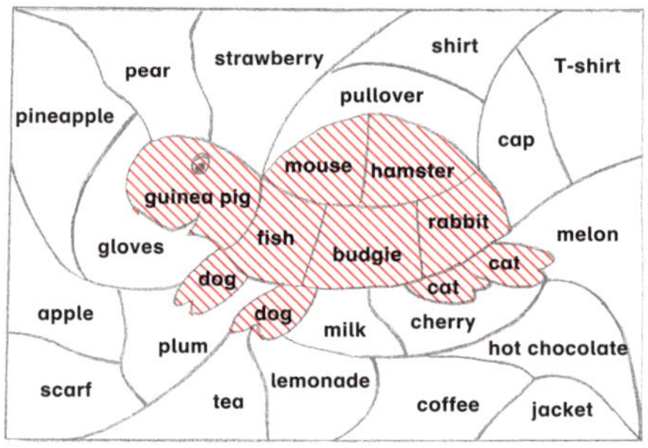

pear   strawberry   shirt   T-shirt
pineapple   pullover   cap
mouse   hamster
guinea pig   rabbit
gloves   fish   budgie   melon
apple   dog   cat
dog   milk   cherry
plum   hot chocolate
scarf   tea   lemonade   coffee   jacket

I can see a __tortoise__ .

3. Guess the pets. Write.

Welche Tiere haben sich hinter der Mauer versteckt? Schreibe sie auf.

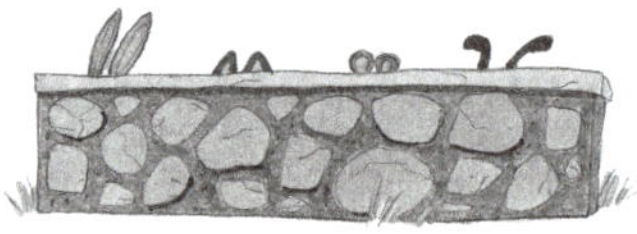

__rabbit, cat, mouse, dog__

39

4. Trace the lines and write.

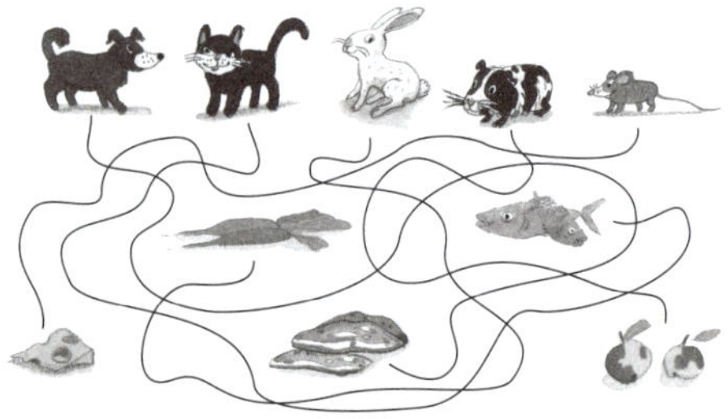

A __dog__ likes ___ . (ham)
A __cat__ likes ___ . (fish)
A __rabbit likes (carrots)__ .
__A guinea pig likes (apples)__ .
__A mouse likes (cheese)__ .

mouse
cat
guinea pig
dog
rabbit

Cheese for you and a lollipop for me.

40

1. Write and draw lines.

Schreibe zuerst unter jedes Bild die passende Jahreszeit. Ordne dann den Jahreszeiten die Monate zu.

spring   summer
autumn   winter

June
May
August
April
July
March

It's __spring__ .   It's __summer__ .

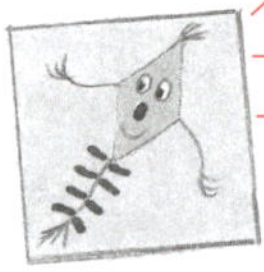

September
January
November
October
February
December

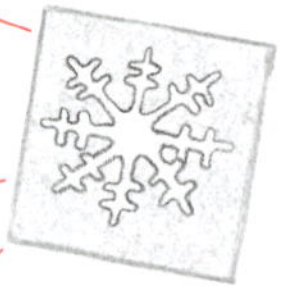

It's __autumn__ .   It's __winter__ .

2. Write the 12 months in the correct order.

1. __January__   2. __February__   3. __March__
4. __April__   5. __May__   6. __June__
7. __July__   8. __August__   9. __September__
10. __October__   11. __November__   12. __December__

41

Our nature

3. Read and tick the correct answer. ✓

Easter is in ...
○ winter ○ summer ✓ spring.

Christmas is in ...
✓ December ○ November ○ September.

Halloween is in ...
○ April ✓ October ○ February.

The summer holidays are in ...
○ January ○ March ✓ July/August.

4. What can you see? Write. ✓

| pond |
| butter-fly |
| tree |
| grass |
| frog |
| flower |

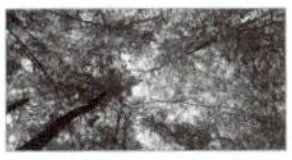

I can see a _tree_ .
I can see a _flower_ . 
I can see a _frog_ . 
I can see a _pond_ . 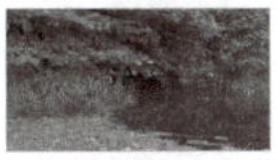
I can see _grass_ . 
I can see a _butterfly_ . 

42

Our nature

5. Find the months. Draw lines and write. ✓

Octo- Novem-
Jul-
Janua-
Mar- -ber
Decem-
Septem-

Welche dieser Monate haben die Endung -ber.

September, October, November, December

6. What can you see?
Colour the spring words green, the summer words yellow, the autumn words brown and the winter words blue.

Christmas · snowman
June
August · summer
January
Sep-tember · February
July · October · pond
Novem-ber · autumn
snow · ffrog
December
winter · March · May
spring · butterfly · April
flower
cold · ice

Male die Frühlingswörter grün, die Sommerwörter gelb, die Herbstwörter braun und die Winterwörter blau an. Und dann lass dich überraschen.

blau
gelb
braun
grün

I can see a _flower_

43

Farm animals

1. These animals live on a farm. Write the words and draw lines. ✓

h ū rs ē
sh ē ē p
c ō w
g ō ō s ē
d ū ck
p ī g
h ē n

horse pig hen sheep goose cow duck

44

Farm animals

2. What do they say? Write. ✓ ?

neigh-neigh
cluck-cluck
honk-honk
moo-moo
oink-oink
baa-baa
quack-quack

Was ist denn hier passiert? Wie muss es richtig heißen? Trage in die Lücken ein.

A _duck_ says quak-quak.
A _hen_ says cluck-cluck.
A _pig_ says oink-oink.
A _horse_ says neigh-neigh.
A _goose_ says honk-honk.
A _sheep_ says baa-baa.
A _cow_ says moo-moo.

duck goose horse pig hen sheep cow

45

Lösungen

3. Read the comic. [?]

On the farm

No, I'm a horse. I like grass.

Do you like my lollipop?

No, I'm a cow. I like grass.

Do you like my lollipop?

No, I'm a sheep. I like grass.

Do you like my lollipop?

I'm a kangaroo and I like lollipops. I'm the only lollipop lady on the farm.

46

1. Colour the British flag – The Union Jack. [✓]

blau

rot

rot

weiß

2. What can you see in the pictures? Write. [✓] [?]

Tower Bridge

London Eye

Buckingham Palace

Big Ben

| Buckingham Palace | Tower Bridge | London Eye | Big Ben |

47

3. Read the comic. [?]

Sally in London

That's fun!

Next stop, London Eye.

Let's go!

Where's Big Ben?

I can't find Tower Bridge.

Next stop, Buckingham Palace.

I'm having tea with the Queen.

48

Hello, my name is Sally. What's your name?

My name is John.

[✓]

morning
afternoon
evening
night

Good morning

Good afternoon

Good evening

Good night

49

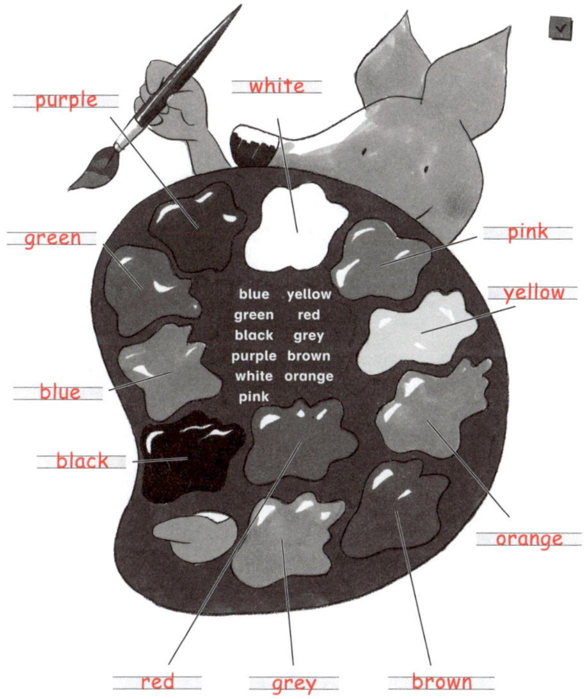

Picture dictionary: Colours

purple
white
green
pink
yellow

blue	yellow
green	red
black	grey
purple	brown
white	orange
pink	

blue
black
orange
red
grey
brown

50

Picture dictionary: Numbers

1 one
2 two
3 three
4 four
5 five
6 six
7 seven
8 eight
9 nine
10 ten

one	two	three	four	five	six	seven
eight	nine	ten				

51

Picture dictionary: At school

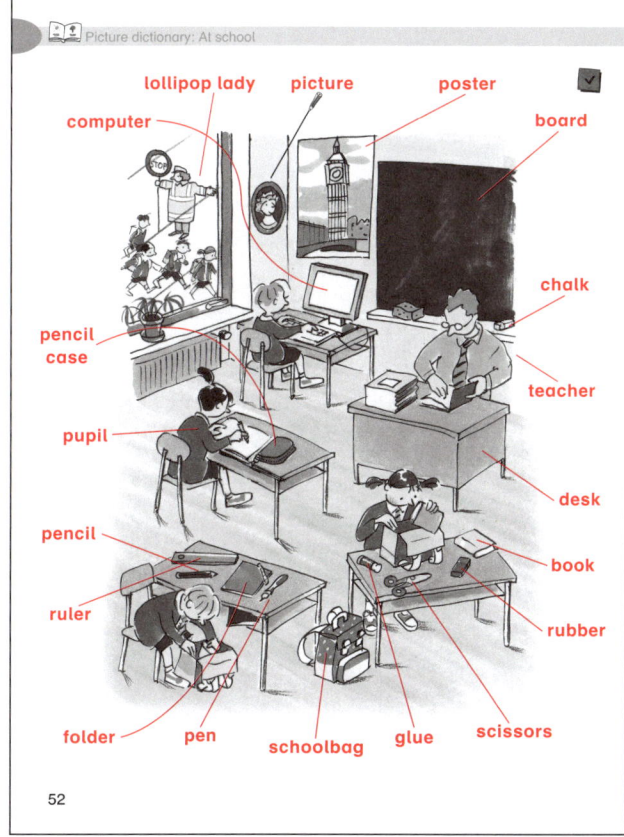

lollipop lady
picture
poster
computer
board
chalk
pencil case
teacher
pupil
desk
pencil
book
ruler
rubber
folder
pen
schoolbag
glue
scissors

52

Picture dictionary: Body and feelings

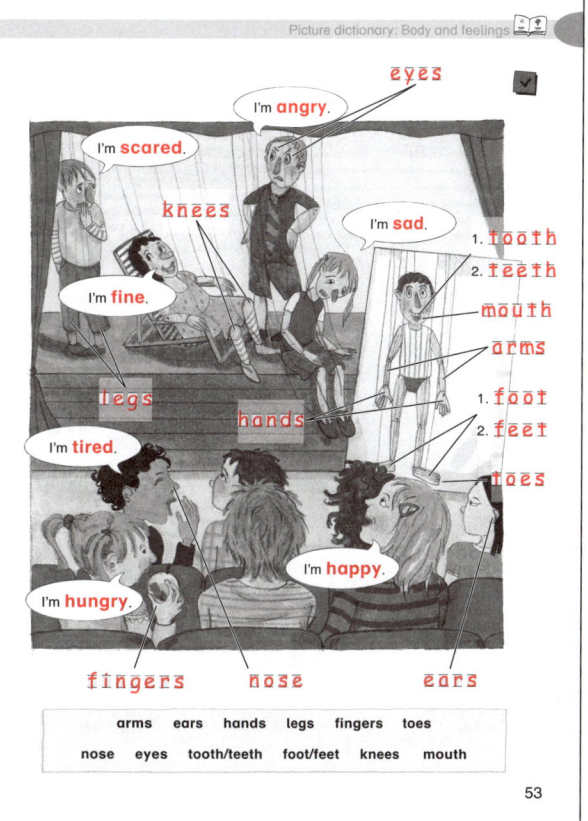

eyes
I'm angry.
I'm scared.
knees
I'm sad.
1. tooth
2. teeth
mouth
arms
I'm fine.
1. foot
2. feet
legs
hands
toes
I'm tired.
I'm happy.
I'm hungry.
fingers
nose
ears

arms	ears	hands	legs	fingers	toes
nose	eyes	tooth/teeth	foot/feet	knees	mouth

53

Lösungen

helicopter

racing car

computer game

doll

teddy bear

spaceship

ball

inline skates

lorry

castle

| racing car | doll | computer game | castle | spaceship |
| ball | helicopter | lorry | inline skates | teddy bear |

shoes

skirt

jacket

shirt

socks

T-shirt

boots

cap

dress

gloves

pullover

scarf

woolly hat

anorak

a pair of trousers

a pair of shorts

It's windy.

It's foggy.

It's rainy.

It's cloudy.

It's sunny and hot.

It's snowy and cold.

1. Monday

2. Tuesday

3. Wednesday

4. Thursday

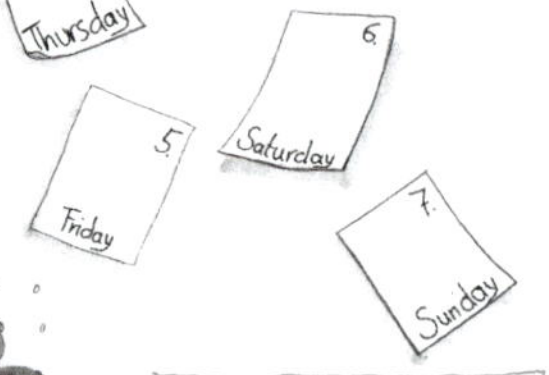

5. Friday

6. Saturday

7. Sunday

sunny	rainy	snowy
cloudy	foggy	windy
	cold	hot

1. father
2. dad

1. mother
2. mum

brother

sister

aunt

1. grandmother
2. grandma

uncle

1. grandfather
2. grandpa

| grandmother/grandma | aunt | father/dad | uncle | sister |
| mother/mum | brother | grandfather/grandpa | | |

hot chocolate
coke
water
orange juice
lemonade
tea
coffee
apple juice
milk

hot chocolate	coffee
tea	milk	coke
orange juice	lemonade
water	apple juice

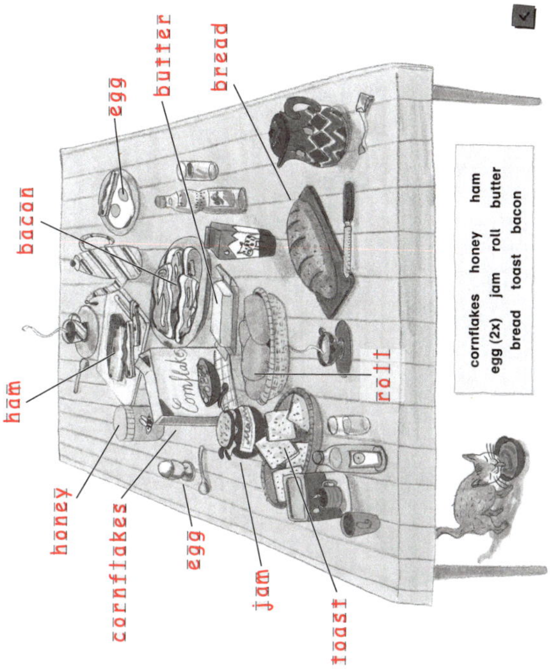

58

egg
butter
bread
bacon
ham
honey
cornflakes
egg
jam
toast
roll

cornflakes	honey		ham
egg (2x)	jam	roll	butter
	bread	toast	bacon

59

lemon
melon
apple
banana
cherry
orange
plum
pear
strawberry
pineapple

melon	lemon	banana
plum	cherry	orange
strawberry	pear
apple	pineapple

60

dog
fish
rabbit
tortoise
mouse
budgie
hamster
cat
guinea pig

| budgie | tortoise | hamster | cat | guinea pig | dog |
| rabbit | mouse | fish |

61

Lösungen

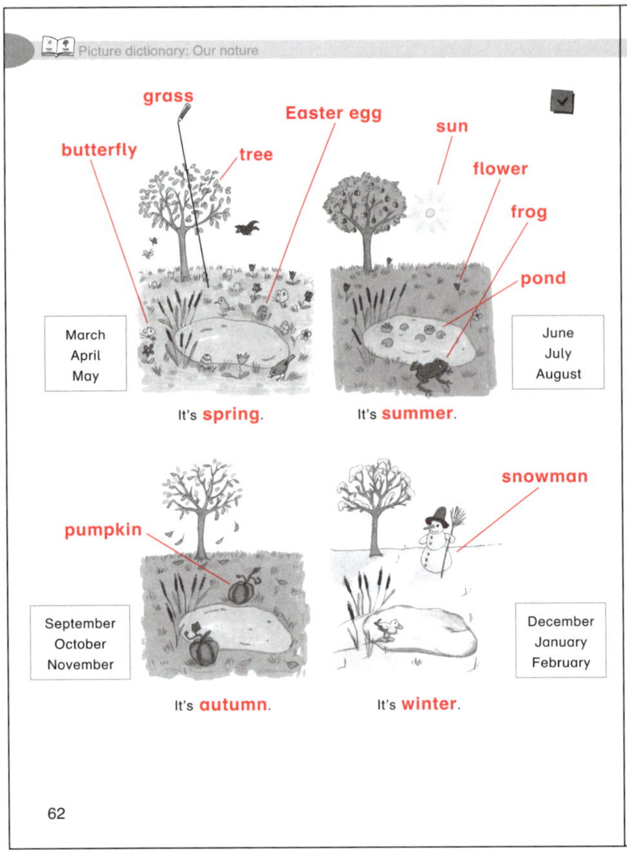
Picture dictionary: Our nature
grass
Easter egg
sun
butterfly
tree
flower
frog
pond
March
April
May
June
July
August
It's spring.
It's summer.
snowman
pumpkin
September
October
November
December
January
February
It's autumn.
It's winter.
62

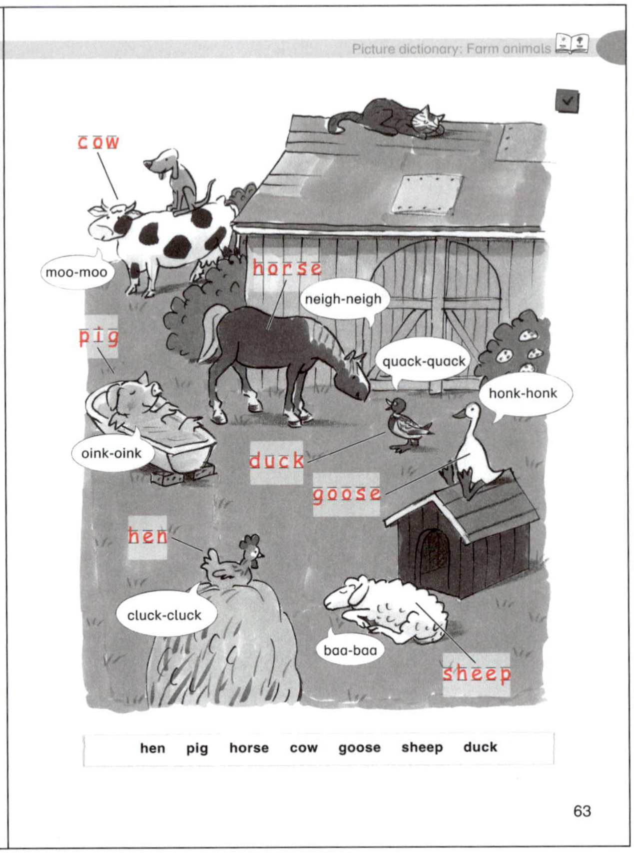
Picture dictionary: Farm animals
cow
moo-moo
horse
neigh-neigh
pig
quack-quack
honk-honk
oink-oink
duck
goose
hen
cluck-cluck
baa-baa
sheep
hen pig horse cow goose sheep duck
63

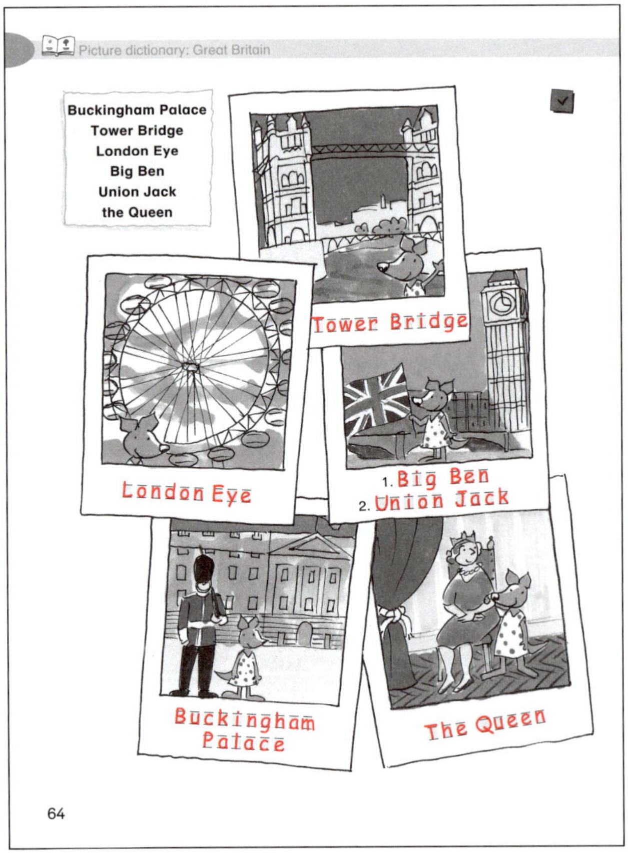
Picture dictionary: Great Britain
Buckingham Palace
Tower Bridge
London Eye
Big Ben
Union Jack
the Queen
Tower Bridge
London Eye
1. Big Ben
2. Union Jack
Buckingham Palace
The Queen
64

Die Lösung zur Seite 3:

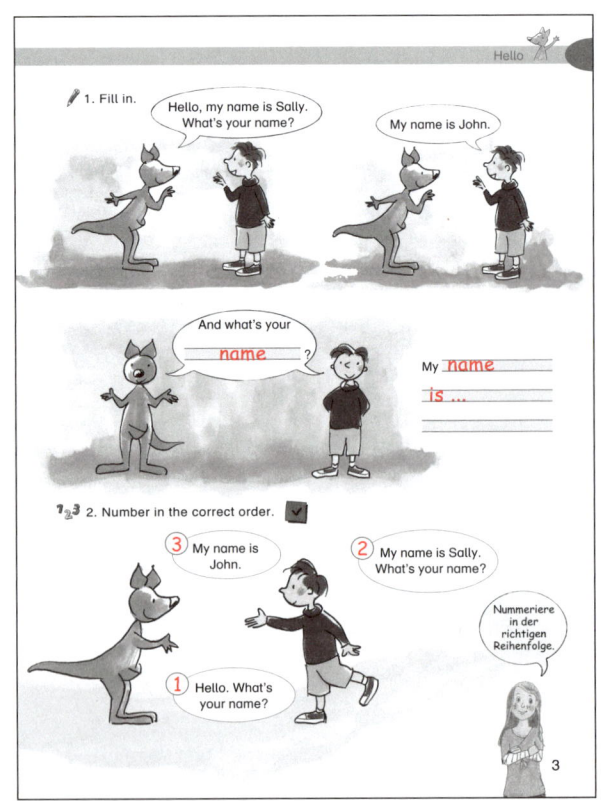

Hello
1. Fill in.
Hello, my name is Sally. What's your name?
My name is John.
And what's your name?
My name is ...
2. Number in the correct order.
3 My name is John.
2 My name is Sally. What's your name?
1 Hello. What's your name?
Nummeriere in der richtigen Reihenfolge.
3

3. Read and draw lines.

I like cornflakes with milk for breakfast.

I like a roll with jam and hot chocolate for breakfast.

I like bacon and eggs and orange juice for breakfast.

I like toast with honey and milk for breakfast.

4. What's missing? Read and draw.

I have toast with jam and a glass of orange juice for breakfast.

I have a roll with ham and a glass of milk for breakfast.

I have bread with butter, an egg and a cup of tea for breakfast.

Ergänze die Bilder.

33

1 2 3 5. Read and number. ✔ ?

Findest du heraus, wer an welchem Platz sitzt?

I don't like cornflakes, but I like coffee. ◯

I like toast, but I don't like hot chocolate. ◯

I don't like toast. ◯

I don't like ham. ◯

6. Crazy breakfast. What's wrong? Write. ✔

Irgendwie sind die Sätze durcheinandergeraten. Schreibe sie richtig auf.

 I like a roll with tea and a cup of jam.

_____

_____

 I like toast with cornflakes and honey with milk.

_____

_____

 I like bread with orange juice and a glass of ham.

_____

_____

1. Do the crossword. ✔

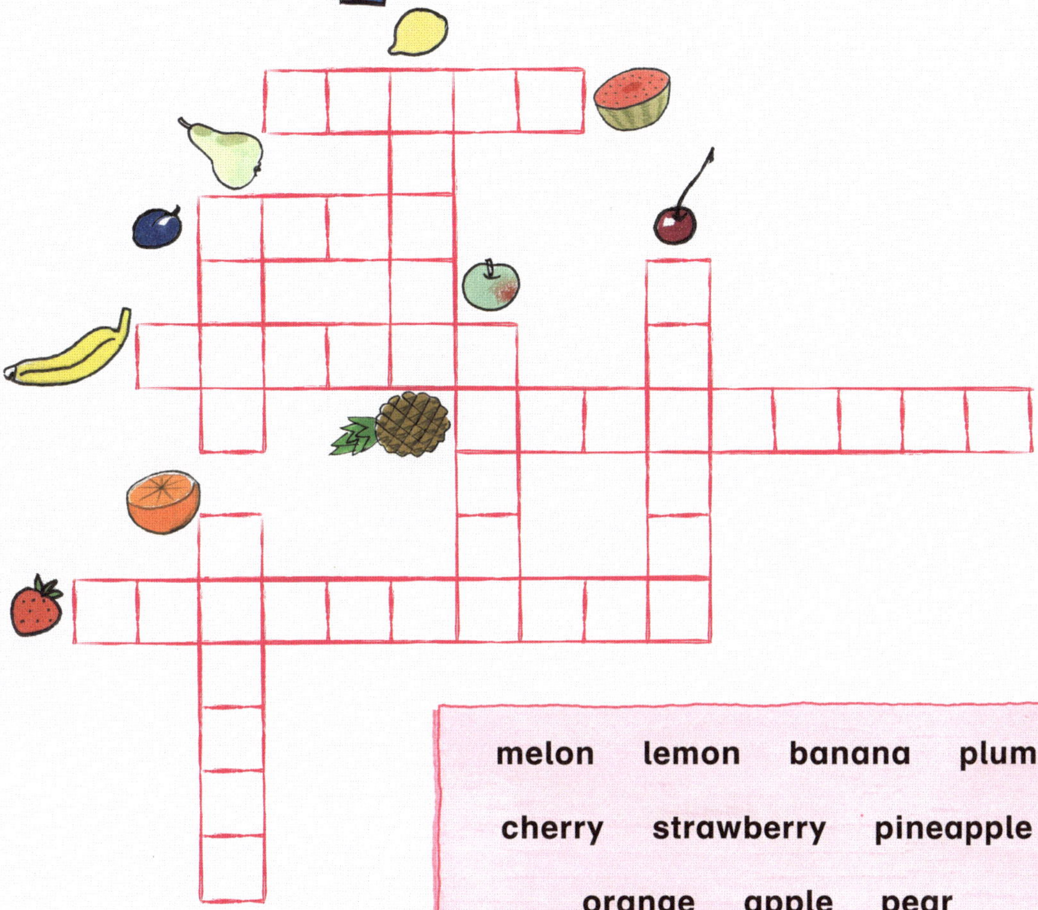

melon   lemon   banana   plum

cherry   strawberry   pineapple

orange   apple   pear

2. Find the five fruit in the basket. Write. ✔

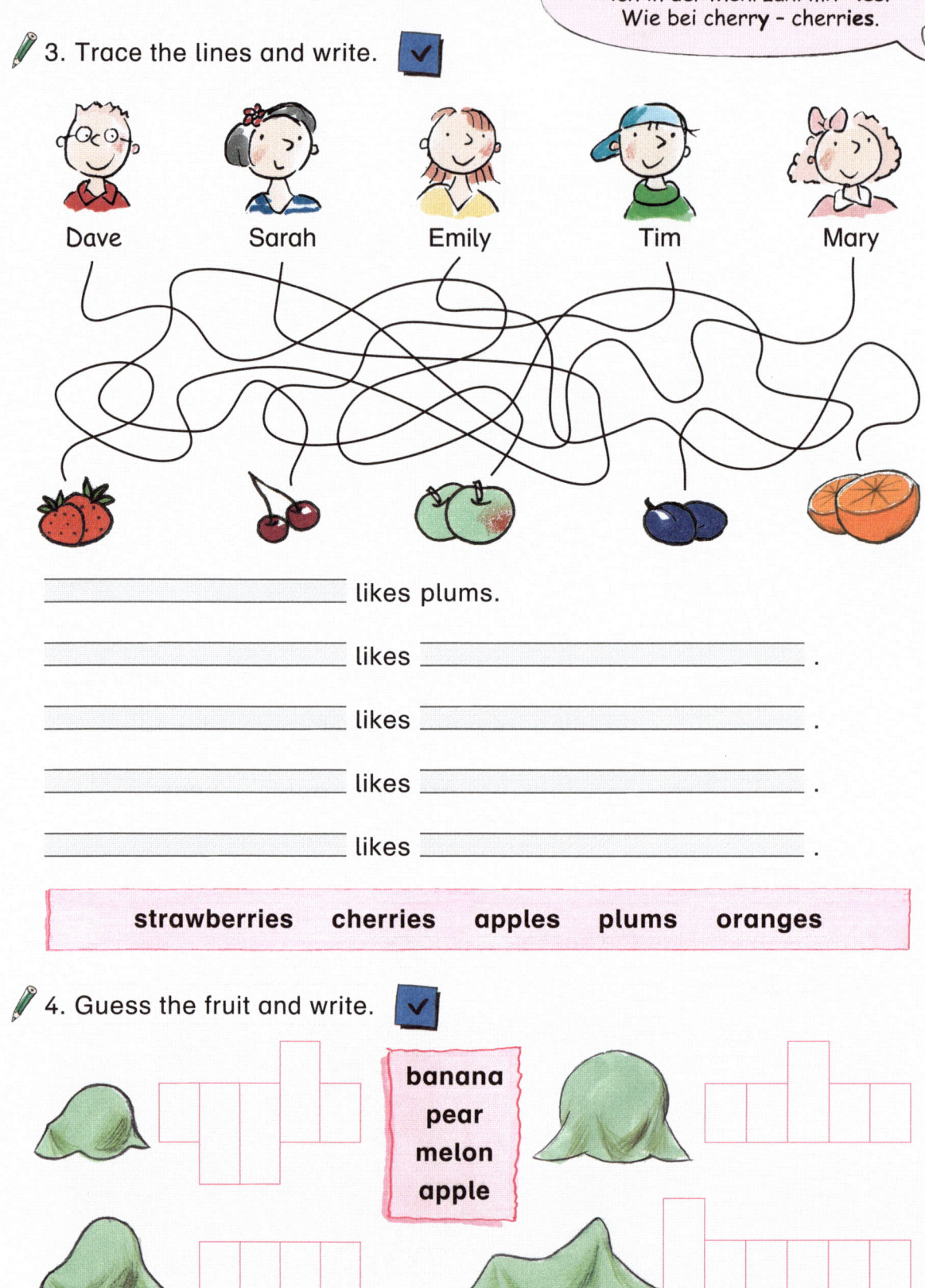

Fruit

Wörter mit **-y** am Ende schreibe ich in der Mehrzahl mit **-ies**. Wie bei cherry – cherr**ies**.

3. Trace the lines and write.

Dave   Sarah   Emily   Tim   Mary

_____ likes plums.

_____ likes _____ .

_____ likes _____ .

_____ likes _____ .

_____ likes _____ .

strawberries   cherries   apples   plums   oranges

4. Guess the fruit and write.

**banana
pear
melon
apple**

36

 5. Read the comic.

Yummy fruit juices

Hello. Would you like a fruit juice?

Hello.

apple juice
lemon juice
pineapple juice
plum juice
strawberry-
banana juice
melon-pear-
juice
orange juice
cherry juice
£1

Yes, an apple juice, please. No, sorry. A strawberry-banana juice, please.

No, sorry! A pineapple juice.

No, sorry! A lemon juice.

You can have a fruit juice with all the fruit.

No, sorry! A plum juice.

That's great!

That's £ 1, please.

Here you are.

Thank you! Yummy! I love this fruit juice!!!

 Pets

1. What pet is it? Write and draw lines. ✔

**budgie   cat
dog   fish
guinea pig
hamster   mouse
rabbit   tortoise**

My pet is red. It can swim.

It's a _____ .

My pet is black. It says "miaow".

It's a _____ .

My pet is blue. It can fly.

It's a _____ .

My pet is brown and white. It's very small.

It's a _____ .

My pet is brown. It says "bow-wow".

It's a _____ .

My pet is black and white. It likes apples.

It's a _____ .

My pet is green. It has got short legs.

It's a _____ .

My pet is white. It has got long ears.

It's a _____ .

And my pet
is a mouse.

 **2.** Find the pets and colour the fields green.
What can you see?

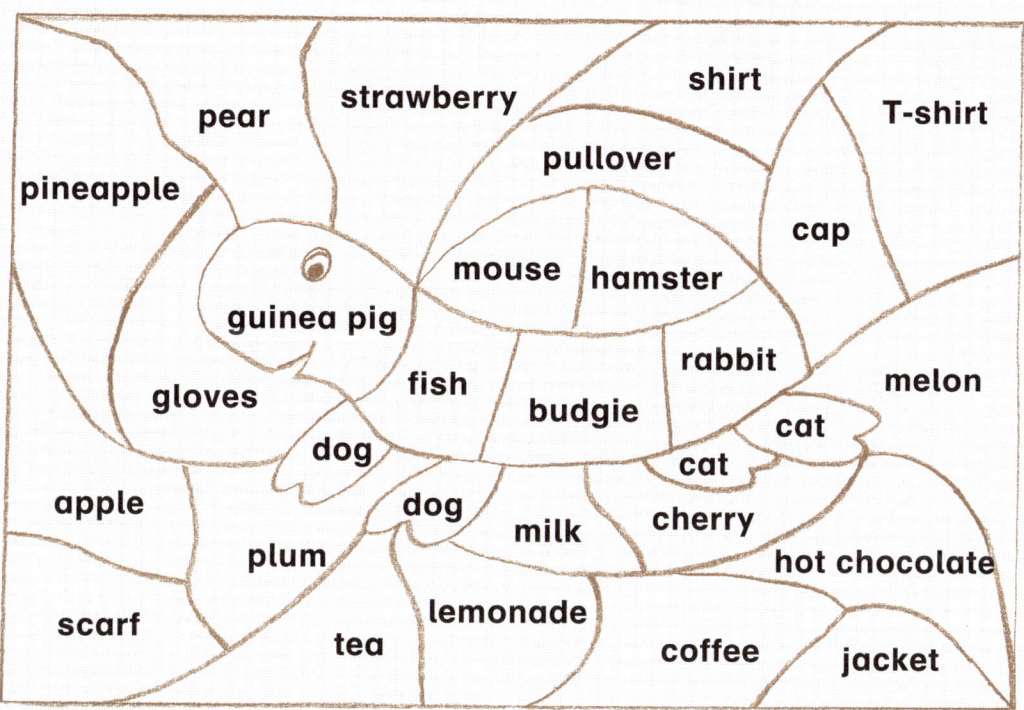

- shirt
- pear
- strawberry
- T-shirt
- pullover
- pineapple
- cap
- mouse
- hamster
- guinea pig
- rabbit
- melon
- gloves
- fish
- budgie
- cat
- dog
- cat
- apple
- dog
- milk
- cherry
- plum
- hot chocolate
- scarf
- lemonade
- tea
- coffee
- jacket

 I can see a _____ .

 3. Guess the pets. Write.

Welche Tiere haben sich hinter der Mauer versteckt? Schreibe sie auf.

_____

39

4. Trace the lines and write. ✔

A _____ likes [meat] .

A _____ likes [fish] .

A _____ [carrot] .

_____ [apples] .

_____ [cheese] .

mouse

cat

guinea pig

dog

rabbit

Cheese for you
and a lollipop for me.

1. Write and draw lines.

Schreibe zuerst unter jedes Bild die passende Jahreszeit. Ordne dann den Jahreszeiten die Monate zu.

spring	summer
autumn	winter

June

May

August

April

July

March

It's _____.

September

January

November

October

February

It's _____.

December

It's _____.

It's _____.

2. Write the 12 months in the correct order.

1. _____ 2. _____ 3. _____

4. _____ 5. _____ 6. _____

7. _____ 8. _____ 9. _____

10. _____ 11. _____ 12. _____

41

3. Read and tick the correct answer. ✔

Easter is in ...

○ winter   ○ summer   ○ spring.

Christmas is in ...

○ December   ○ November   ○ September.

Halloween is in ...

○ April   ○ October   ○ February.

The summer holidays are in ...

○ January   ○ March   ○ July/August.

4. What can you see? Write. ✔

pond	
butter-fly	
tree	
grass	
frog	
flower	

I can see a _____ .

I can see a _____ .

I can see a _____ .

I can see a _____ .

I can see _____ .

I can see a _____ .

5. Find the months. Draw lines and write.

Octo-   Novem-

Jul-

Janua-

Mar-   **-ber**

Decem-

Septem-

Welche dieser Monate haben die Endung -ber.

_____

_____

_____

_____

6. What can you see?
Colour the spring words green, the summer words yellow, the autumn words brown and the winter words blue.

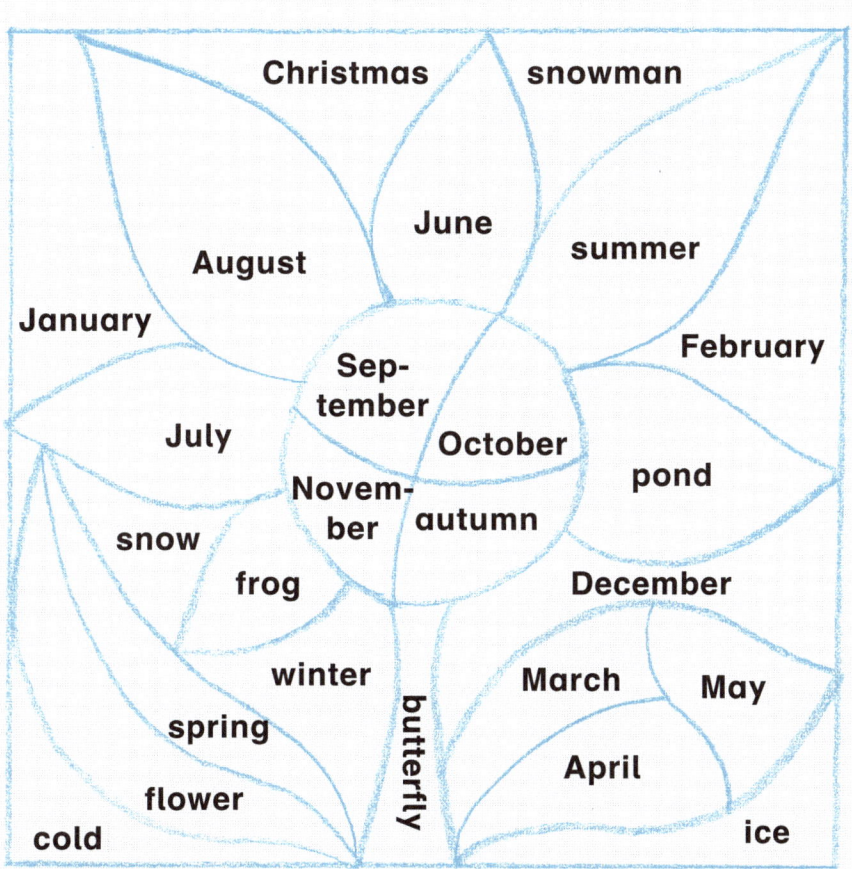

Christmas   snowman

June

August   summer

January

September   February

July   October

November   pond

autumn

snow

frog   December

winter   March   May

spring

butterfly   April

flower

cold   ice

Male die Frühlingswörter grün, die Sommerwörter gelb, die Herbstwörter braun und die Winterwörter blau an. Und dann lass dich überraschen.

I can see a _____ .

✏️ 1. These animals live on a farm. Write the words and draw lines.

h ⬜ rs ⬜

c ⬜ w

sh ⬜ ⬜ p

d ⬜ ck

g ⬜ ⬜ s ⬜

p ⬜ g

h ⬜ n

| horse | pig | hen | sheep | goose | cow | duck |

2. What do they say? Write.

neigh-neigh

cluck-cluck

honk-honk

moo-moo

baa-baa

oink-oink

quack-quack

Was ist denn hier passiert? Wie muss es richtig heißen? Trage in die Lücken ein.

A _duck_ says quak-quak.

A _____ says cluck-cluck.

A _____ says oink-oink.

A _____ says neigh-neigh.

A _____ says honk-honk.

A _____ says baa-baa.

A _____ says moo-moo.

duck	goose	horse	pig	hen	sheep	cow

 3. Read the comic.

On the farm

1. Colour the British flag – The Union Jack. ✔

blue

red

red

white

2. What can you see in the pictures? Write. ✔ ?

_____

_____

_____

_____

Buckingham Palace   **Tower Bridge**   **London Eye**   **Big Ben**

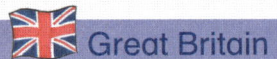

 3. Read the comic.

Sally in London

49

blue   yellow
green   red
black   grey
purple brown
white   orange
pink

1

□ □ □

2

□ □ □

3

□ □ □ □ □

4

□ □ □ □

5

□ □ □ □

6

□ □ □

7

□ □ □ □ □

8

□ □ □ □ □

9

□ □ □ □

10

□ □ □

one	two	three	four	five	six	seven

eight   nine   ten

51

lollipop lady   picture   poster

computer

board

chalk

pencil
case

teacher

pupil

desk

pencil

book

ruler

rubbe

folder   pen   glue   scissors

schoolbag

I'm angry.

I'm scared.

I'm sad.

1. _ _ _ _

2. _ _ _ _

I'm fine.

I'm tired.

1. _ _ _

2. _ _ _

I'm happy.

I'm hungry.

arms	ears	hands	legs	fingers	toes
nose	eyes	tooth/teeth	foot/feet	knees	mouth

53

racing car   doll   computer game   castle   spaceship

ball   helicopter   lorry   inline skates   teddy bear

jacket

skirt

shirt

T-shirt

shoes

socks

boots

cap

dress

pullover

woolly
hat

scarf

gloves

anorak

a pair of trousers

a pair of shorts

55

It's ☐☐☐☐☐ .

1. Monday

It's ☐☐☐☐☐ .

It's ☐☐☐☐☐ .

2. Tuesday

3. Wednesday

It's ☐☐☐☐☐☐ .

4. Thursday

It's ☐☐☐☐☐ and ☐☐☐ .

5. Friday

6. Saturday

7. Sunday

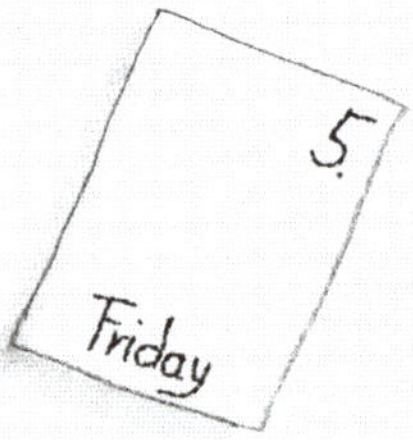

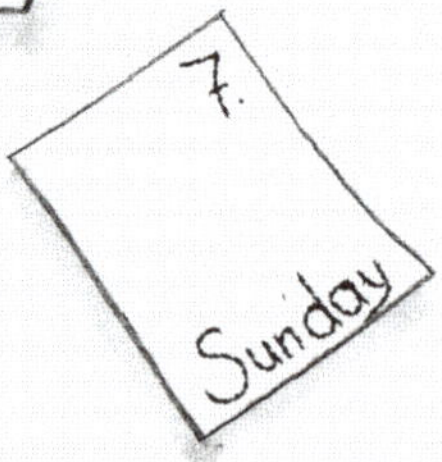

It's ☐☐☐☐☐ and ☐☐☐☐ .

sunny	rainy	snowy
cloudy	foggy	windy
cold	hot

1. ☐☐☐☐☐☐

2. ☐☐☐

1. ☐☐☐☐☐☐☐

2. ☐☐☐

☐☐☐☐☐☐

☐☐☐☐☐☐

☐☐☐☐

1. ☐☐☐☐☐☐☐☐☐☐☐

2. ☐☐☐☐☐☐

☐☐☐☐☐

1. ☐☐☐☐☐☐☐☐☐☐

2. ☐☐☐☐☐☐

grandmother/grandma   aunt   father/dad   uncle   sister
mother/mum   brother   grandfather/grandpa

57

hot chocolate   coffee

tea   milk   coke

orange juice   lemonade

water   apple juice

cornflakes   honey   ham
egg (2x)   jam   roll   butter
bread   toast   bacon

59

melon   lemon   banana

plum   cherry   orange

strawberry   pear

apple   pineapple

open

Pets

budgie   tortoise   hamster   cat   guinea pig   dog

rabbit   mouse   fish

61

grass

Easter egg

sun

butterfly

tree

flower

frog

pond

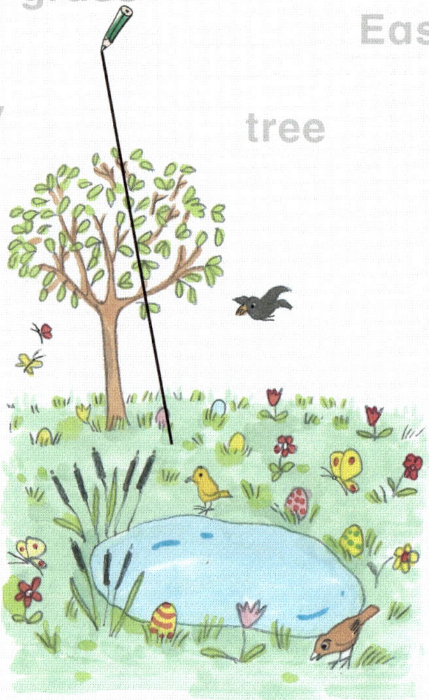

March
April
May

It's spring.

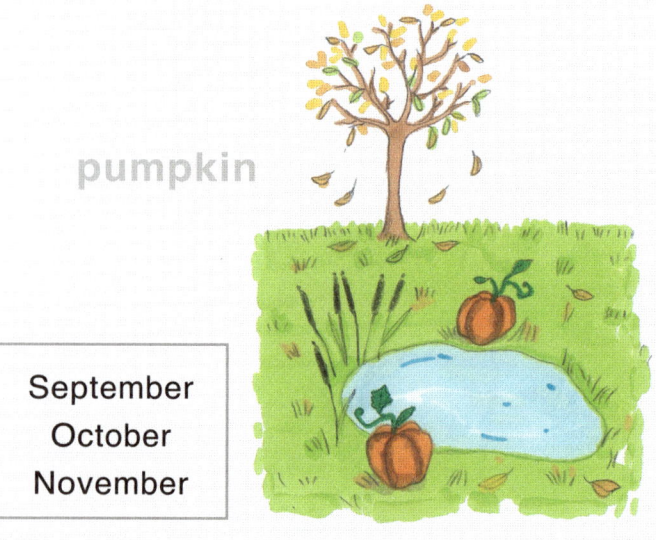

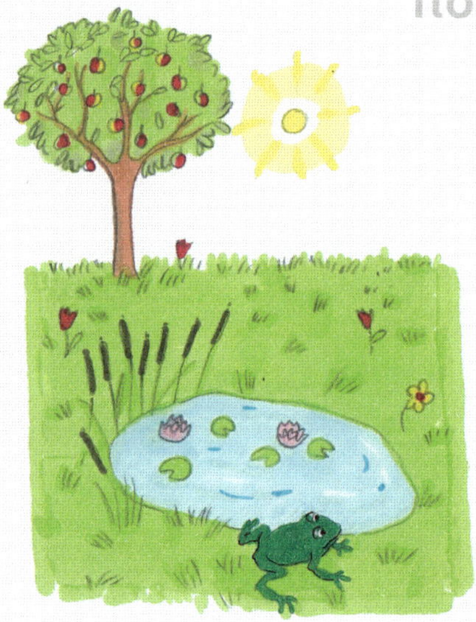

June
July
August

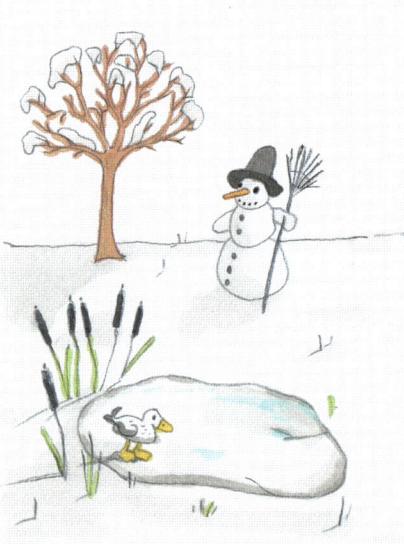

It's summer.

snowman

pumpkin

September
October
November

It's autumn.

December
January
February

It's winter.

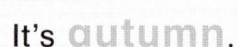

moo-moo

neigh-neigh

quack-quack

honk-honk

oink-oink

cluck-cluck

baa-baa

hen   pig   horse   cow   goose   sheep   duck

Buckingham Palace
Tower Bridge
London Eye
Big Ben
Union Jack
the Queen

1. ▢▢▢ ▢▢▢▢
2. ▢▢▢▢▢▢ ▢▢▢

64